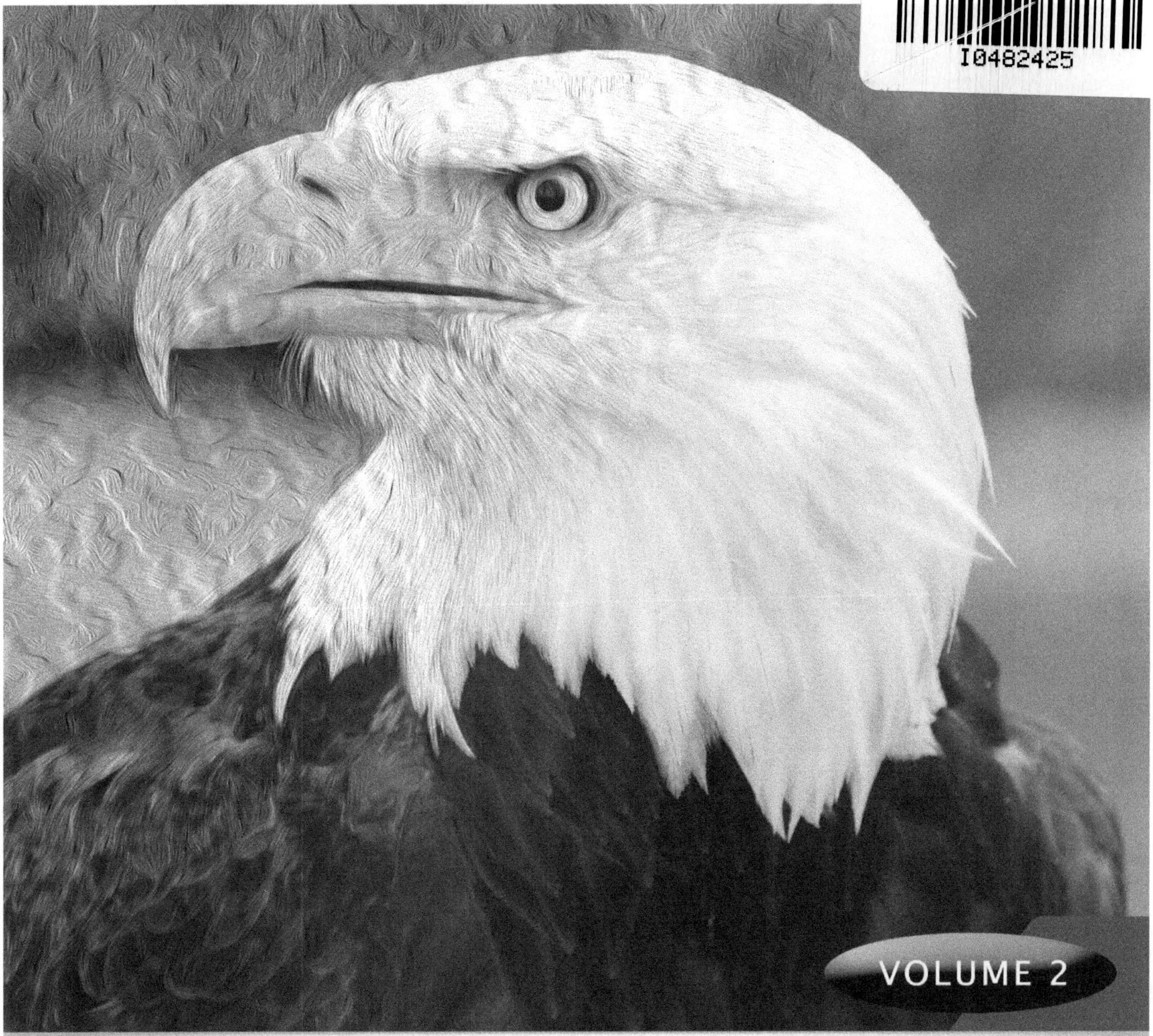

Birdtopia
SHADING

A Grayscale Coloring Book

COLORING BOOK FOR ADULTS

COLOR TEST PAGE

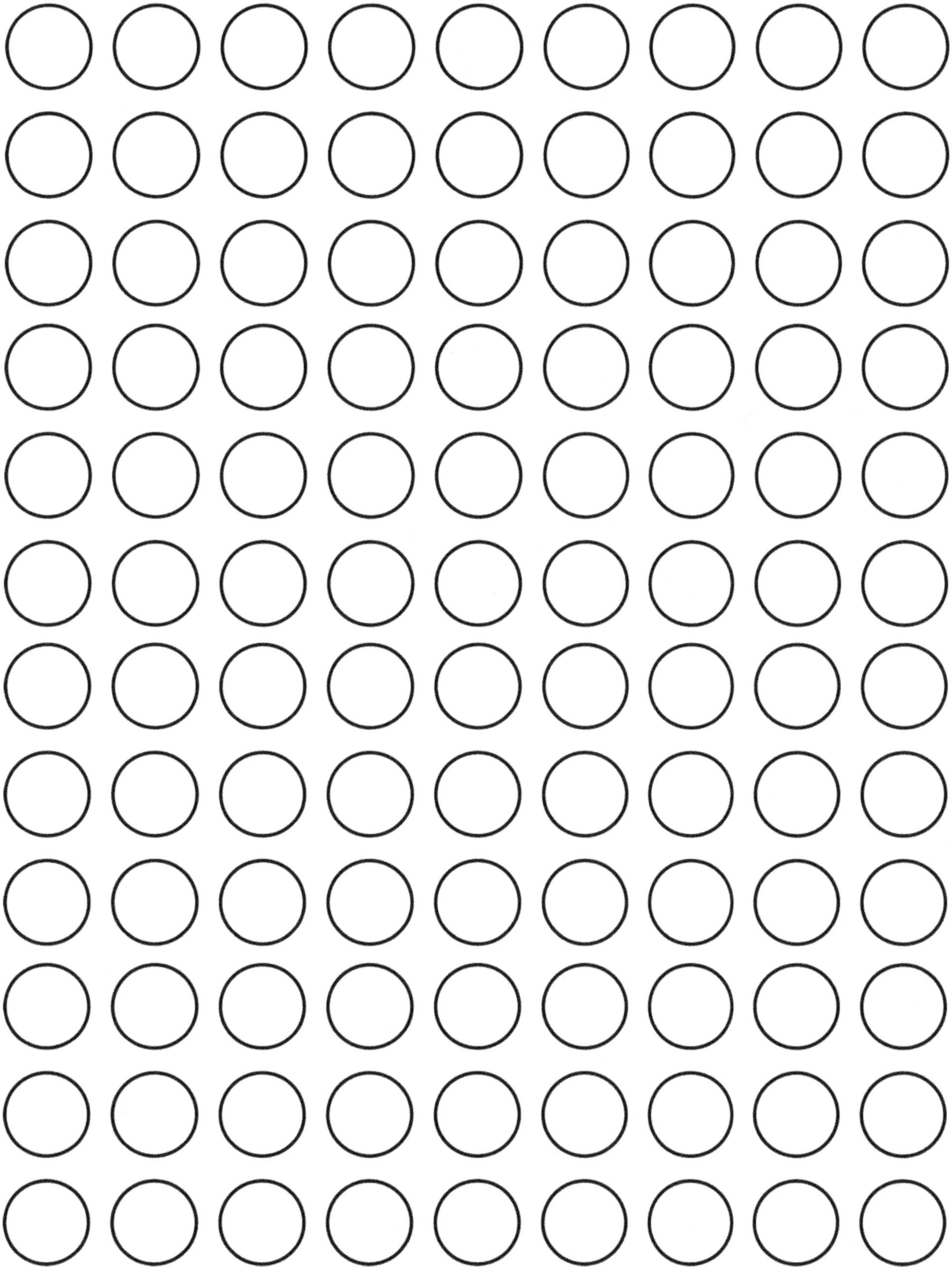

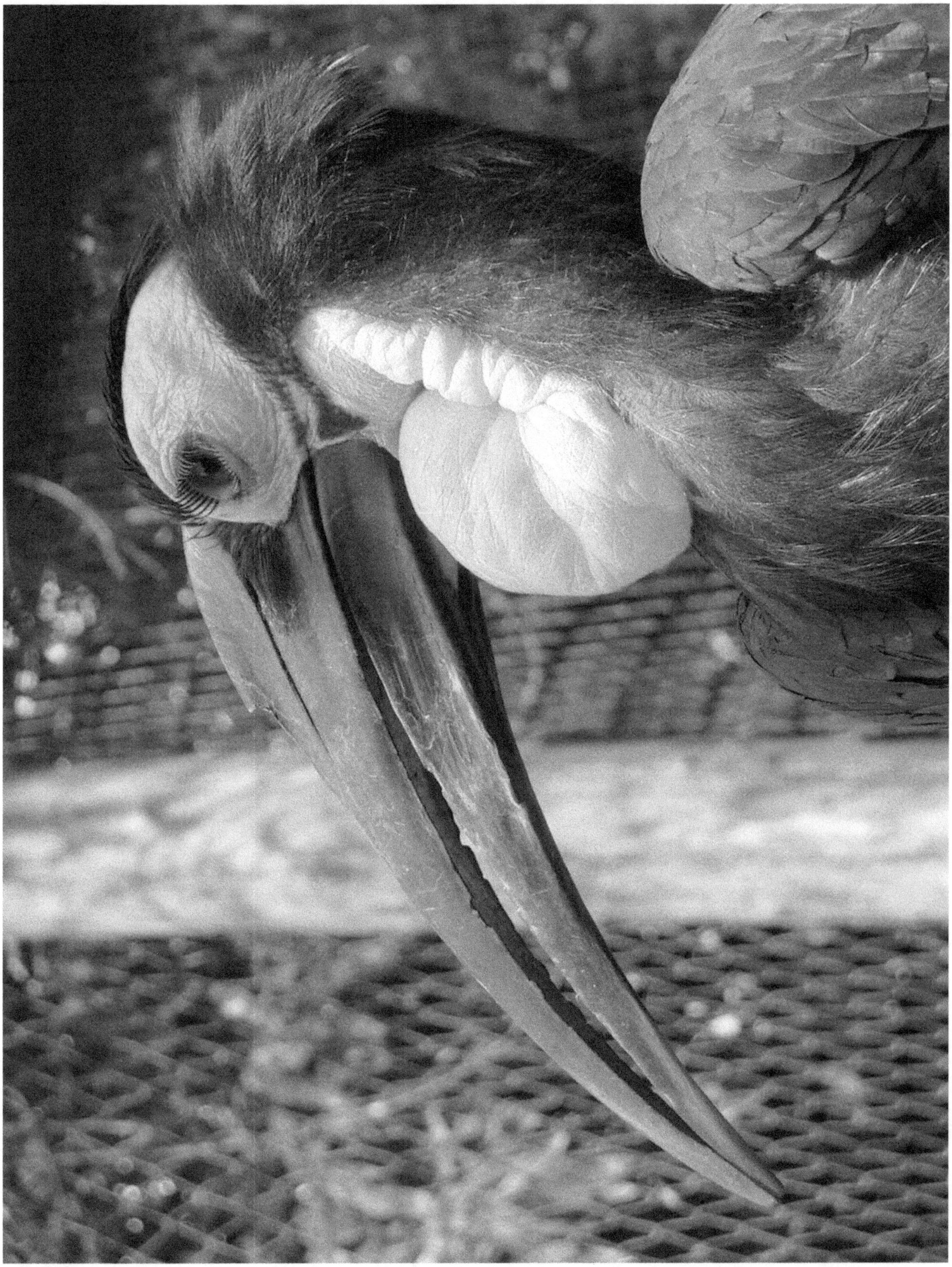

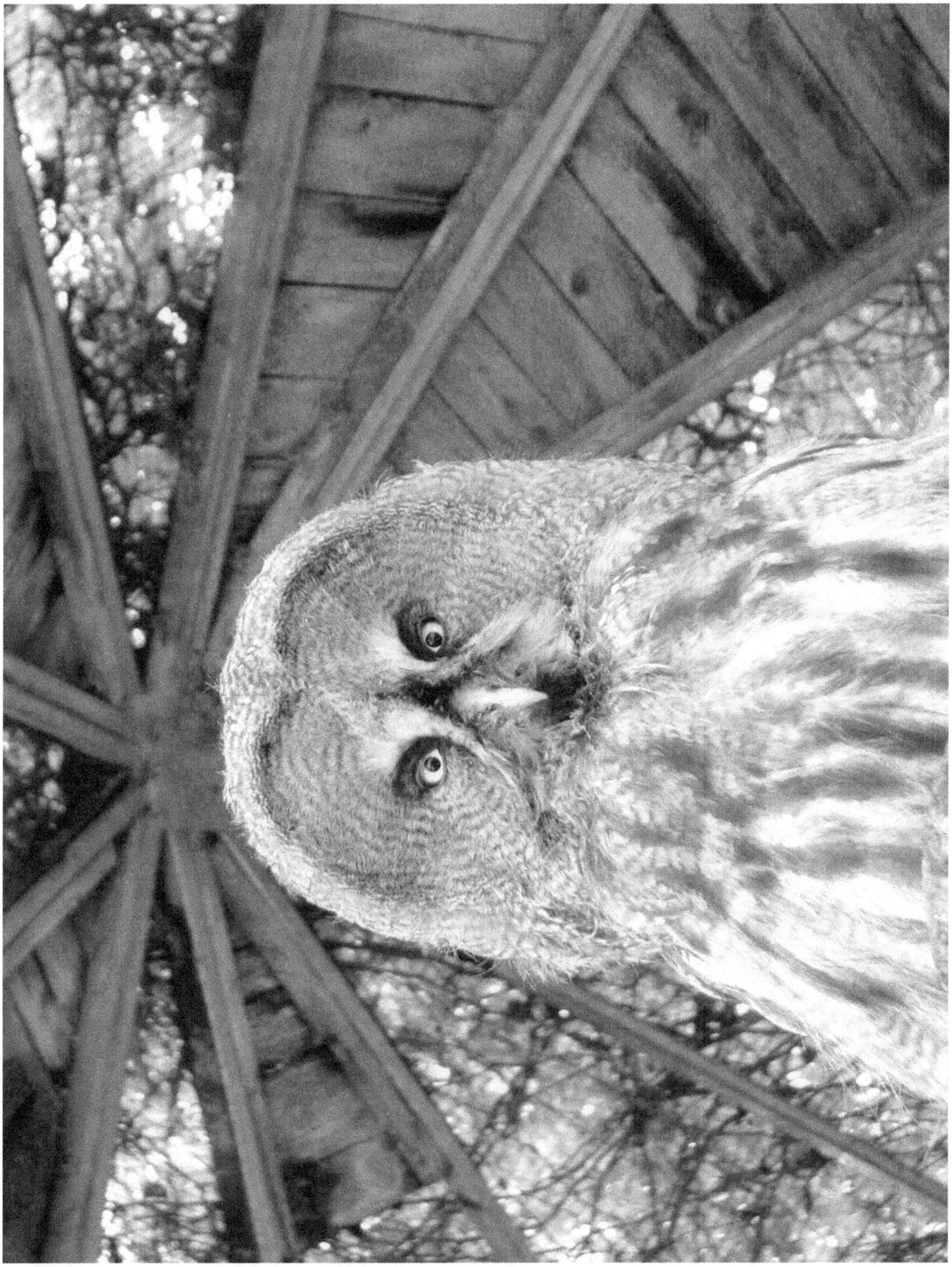

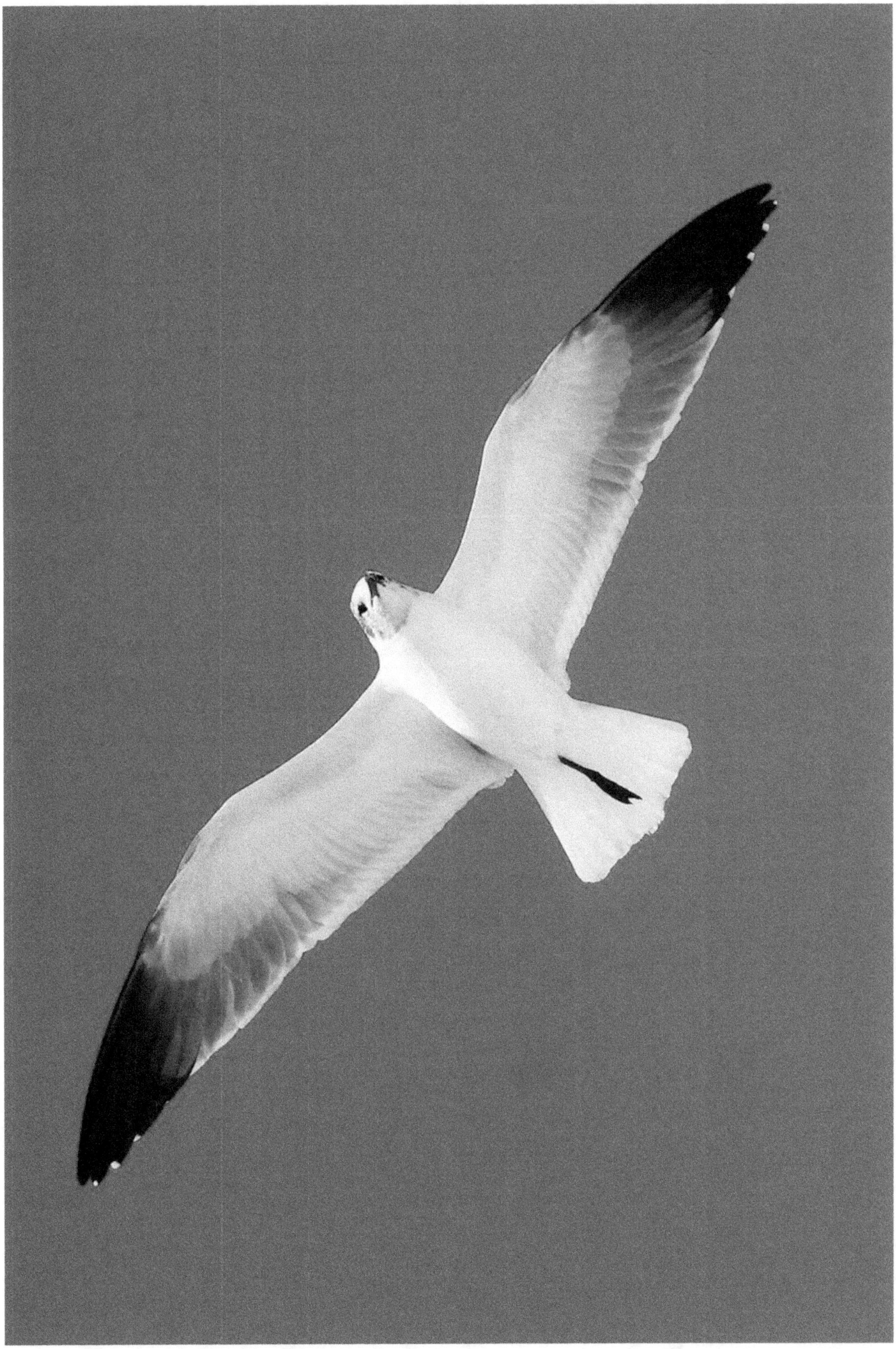

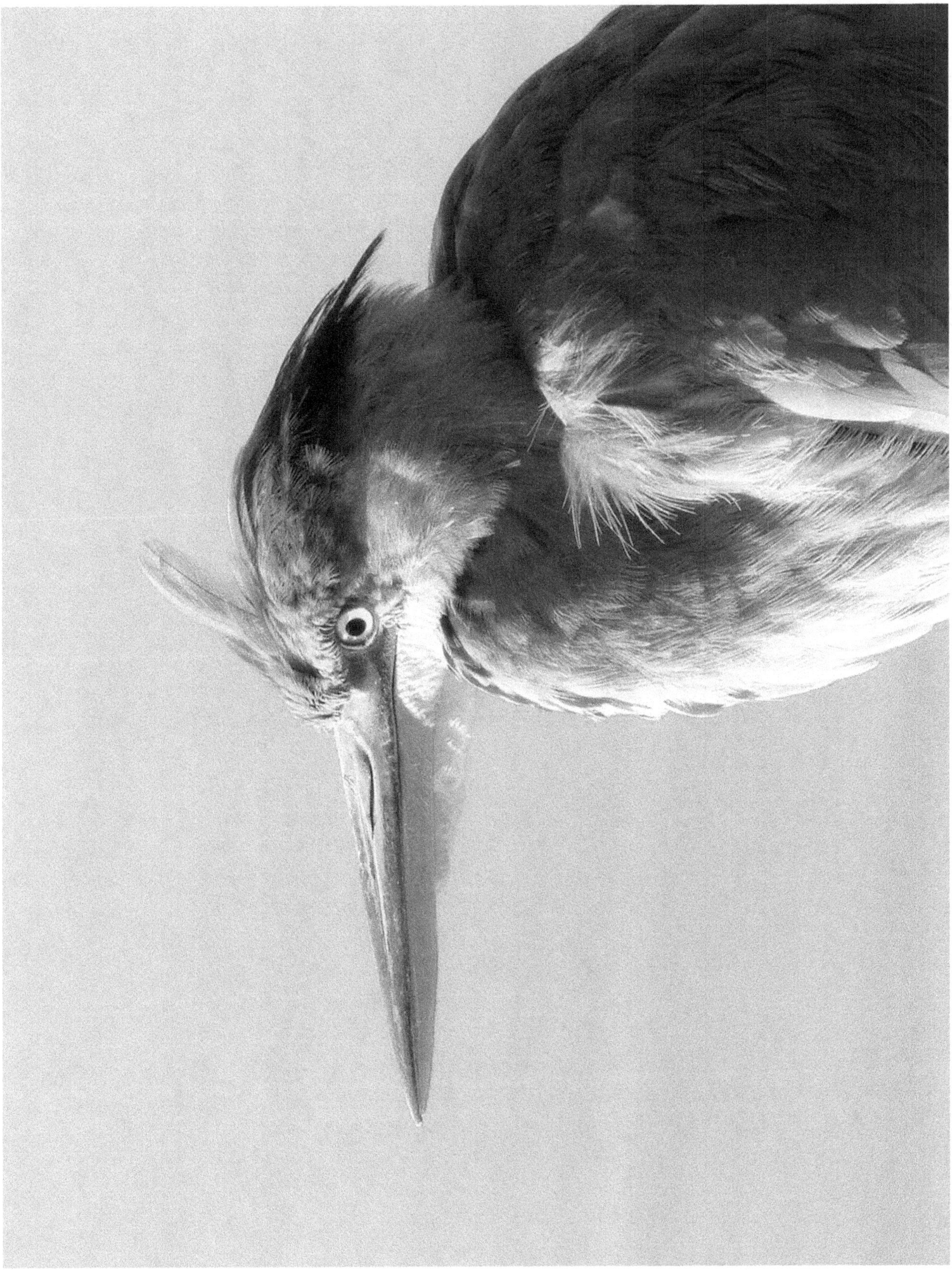

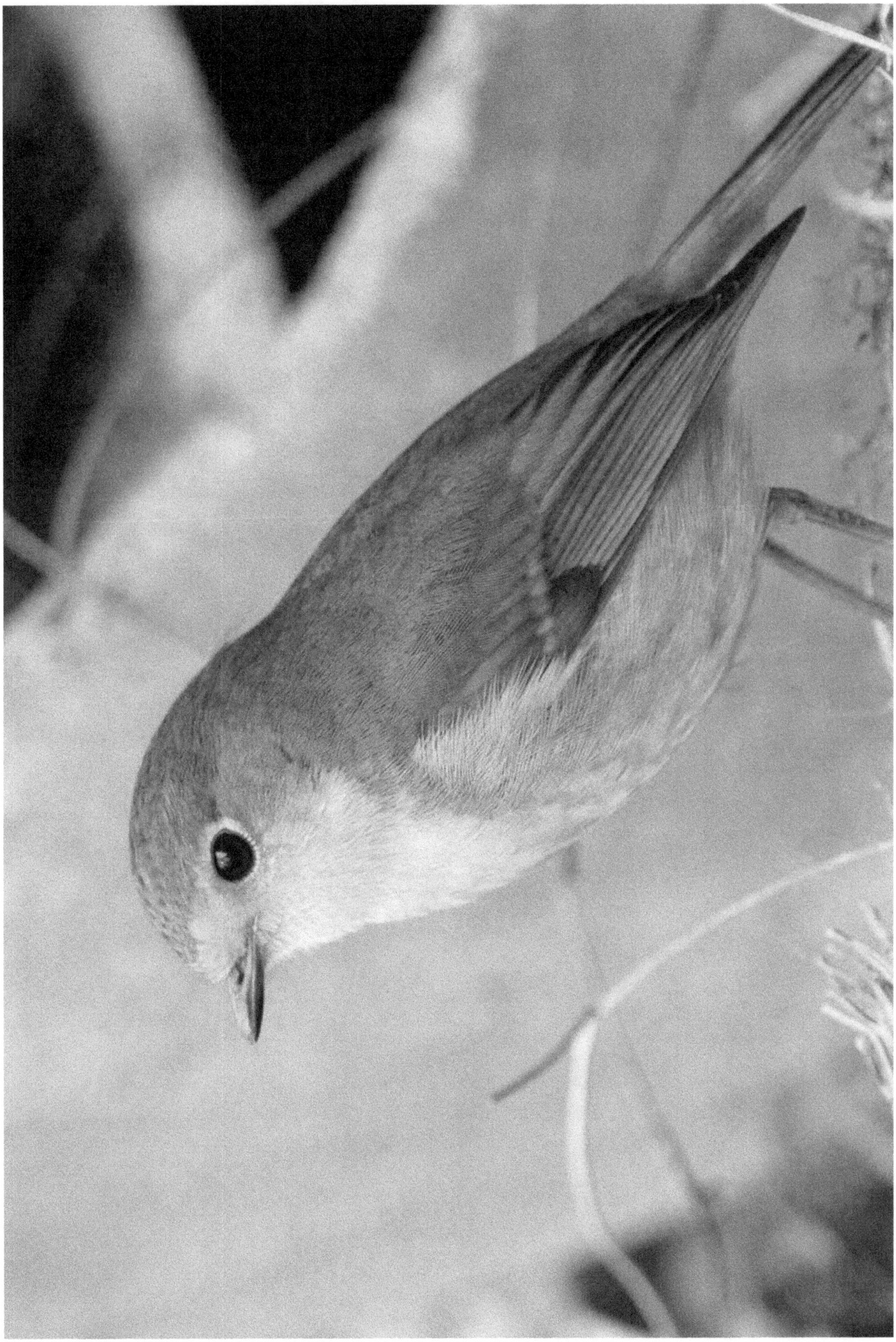

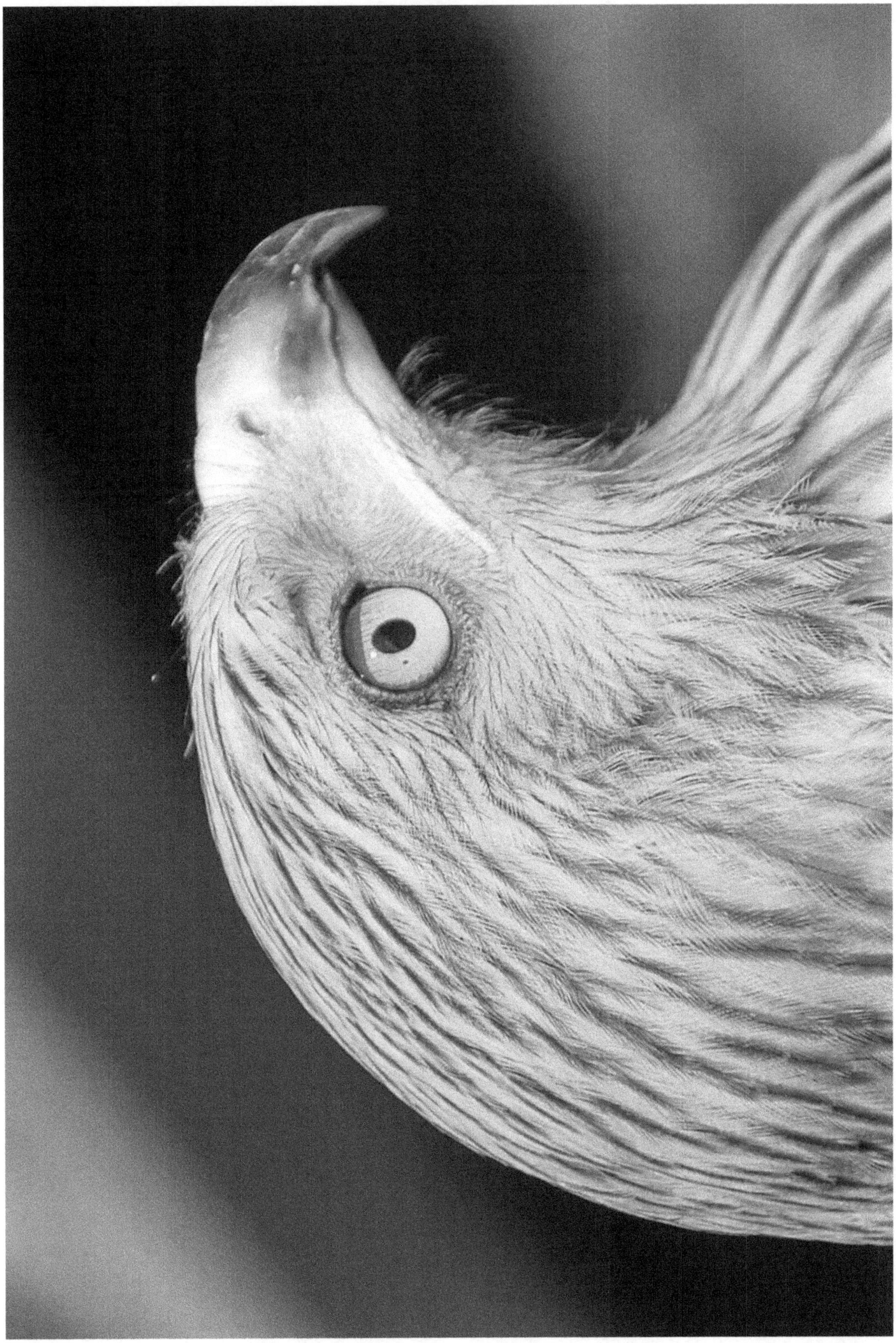

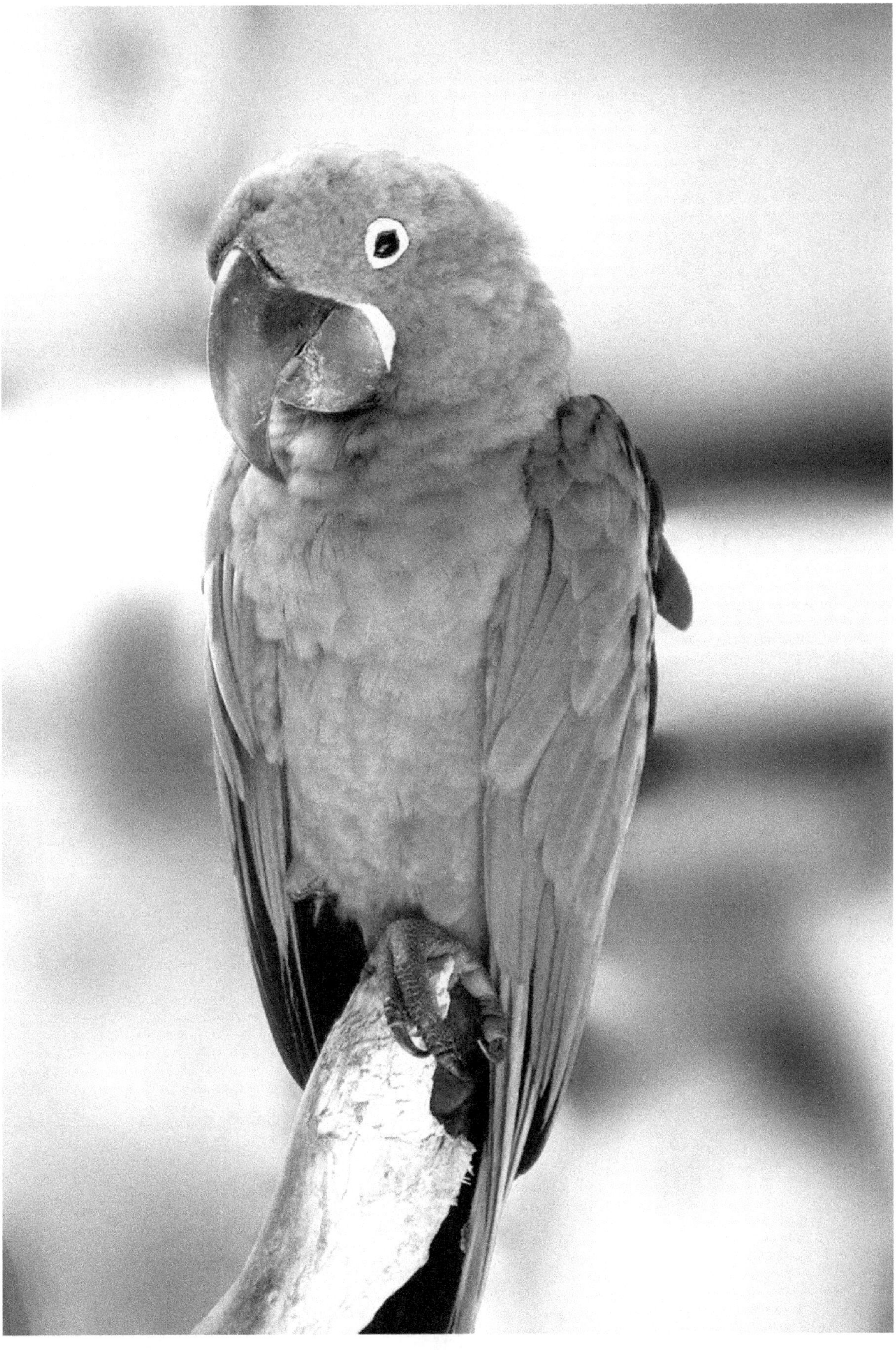

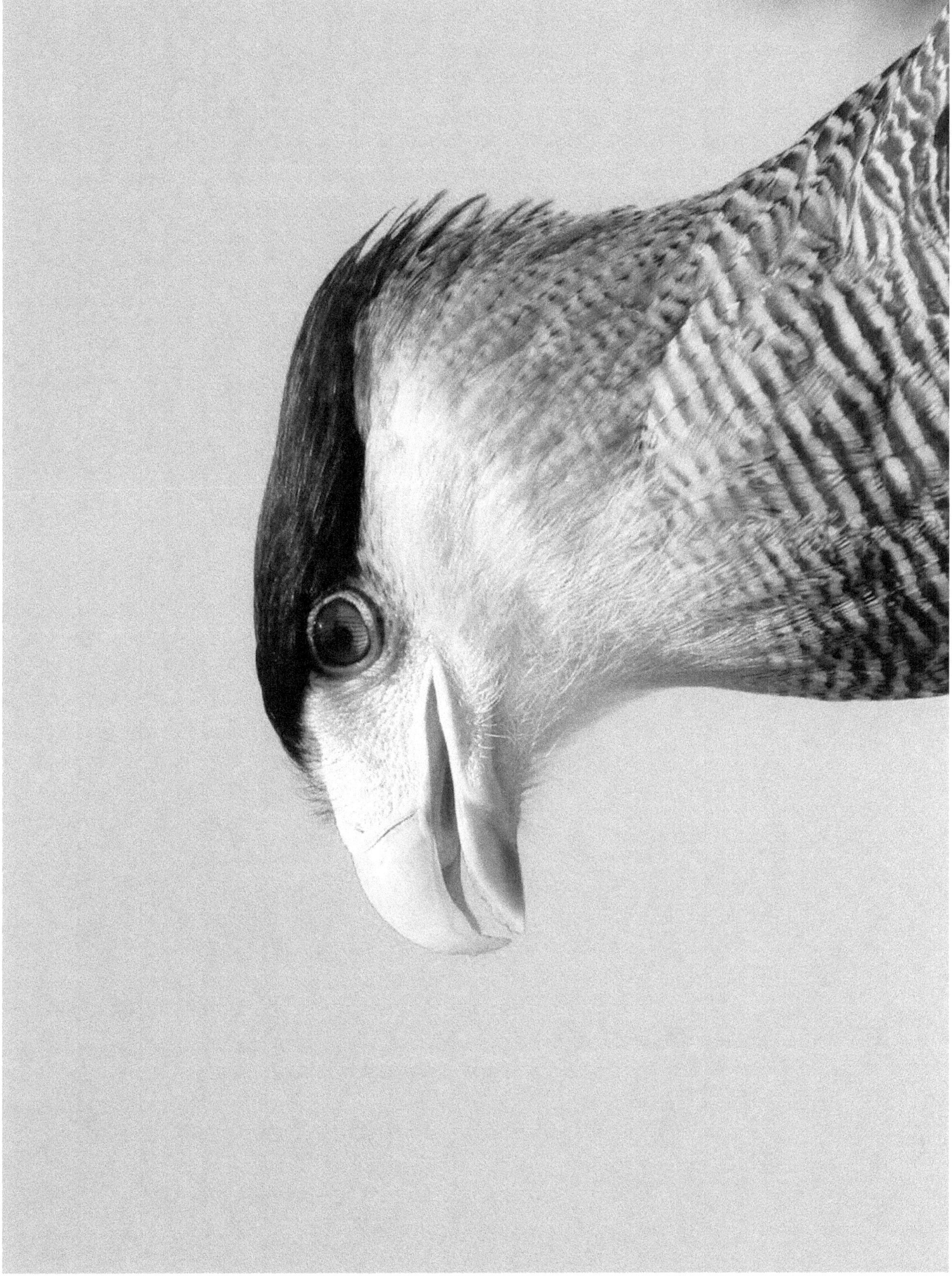

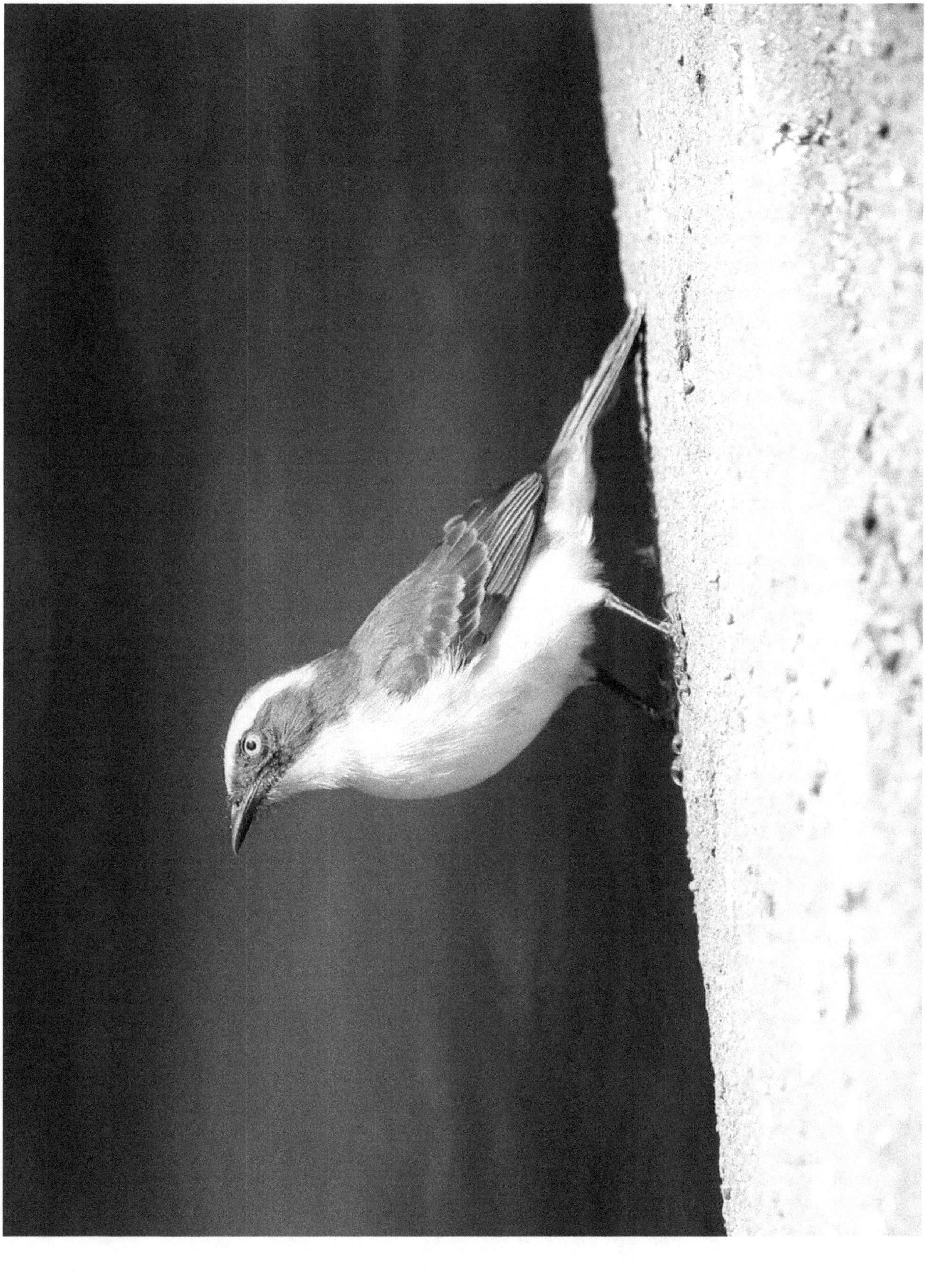

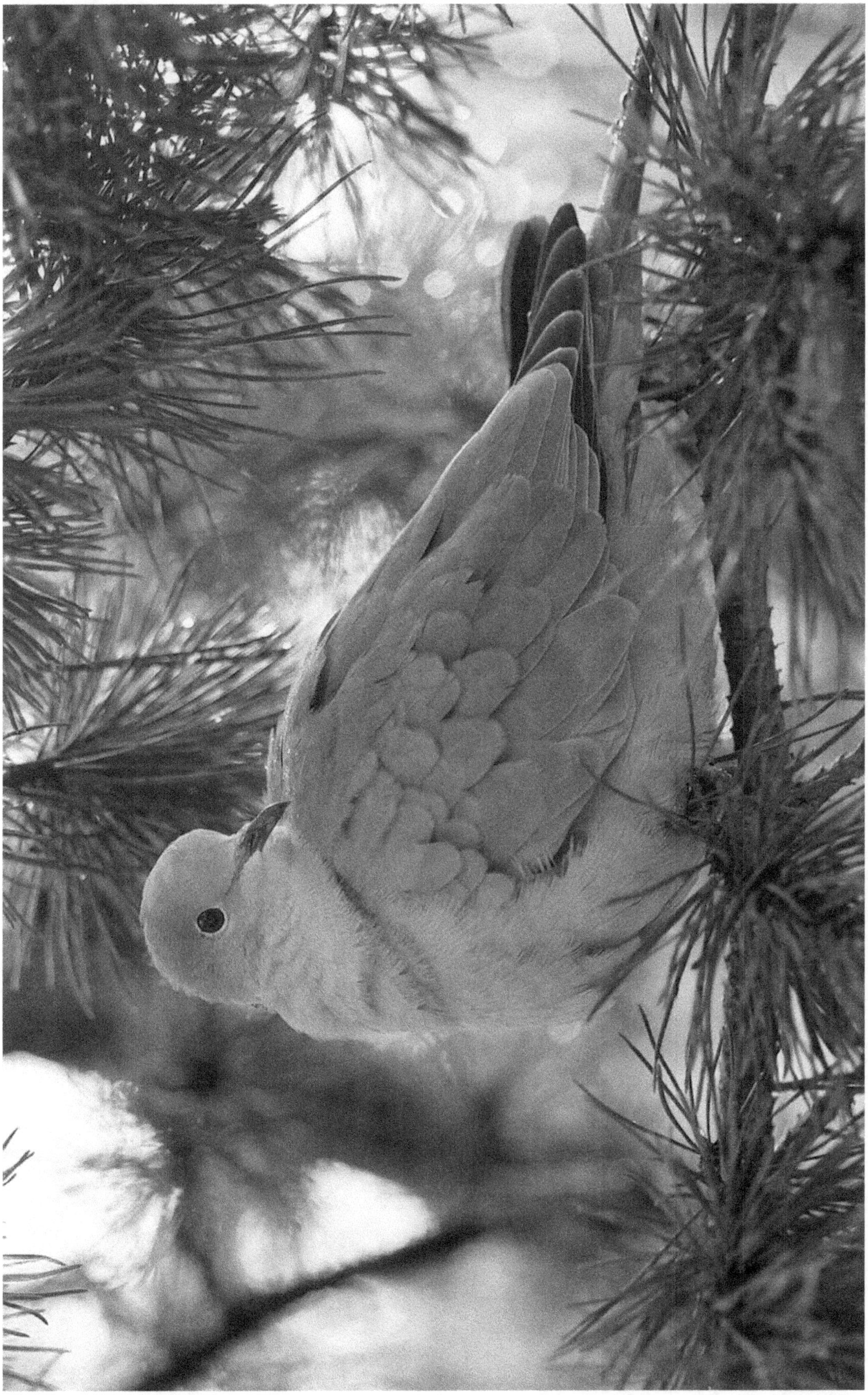

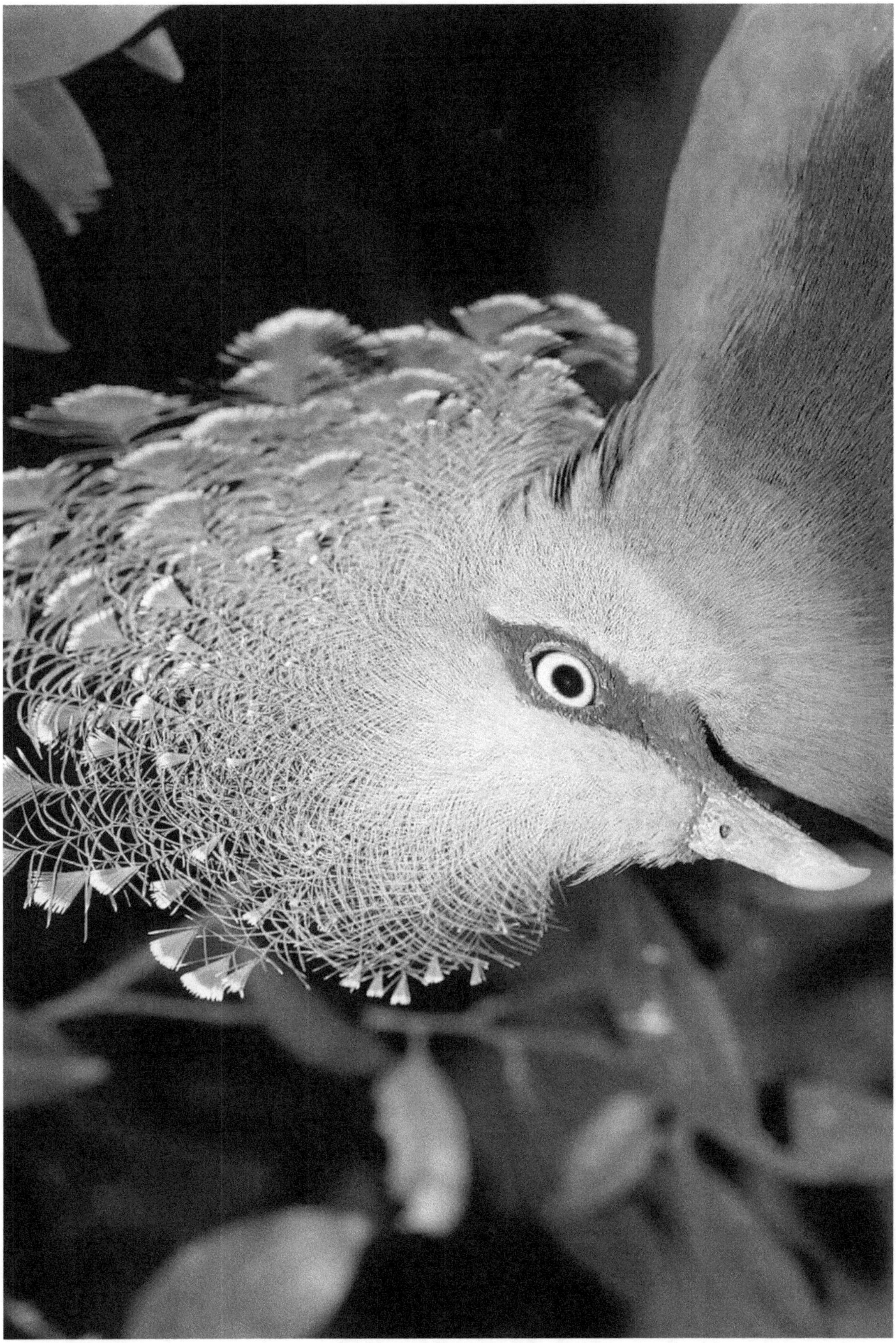

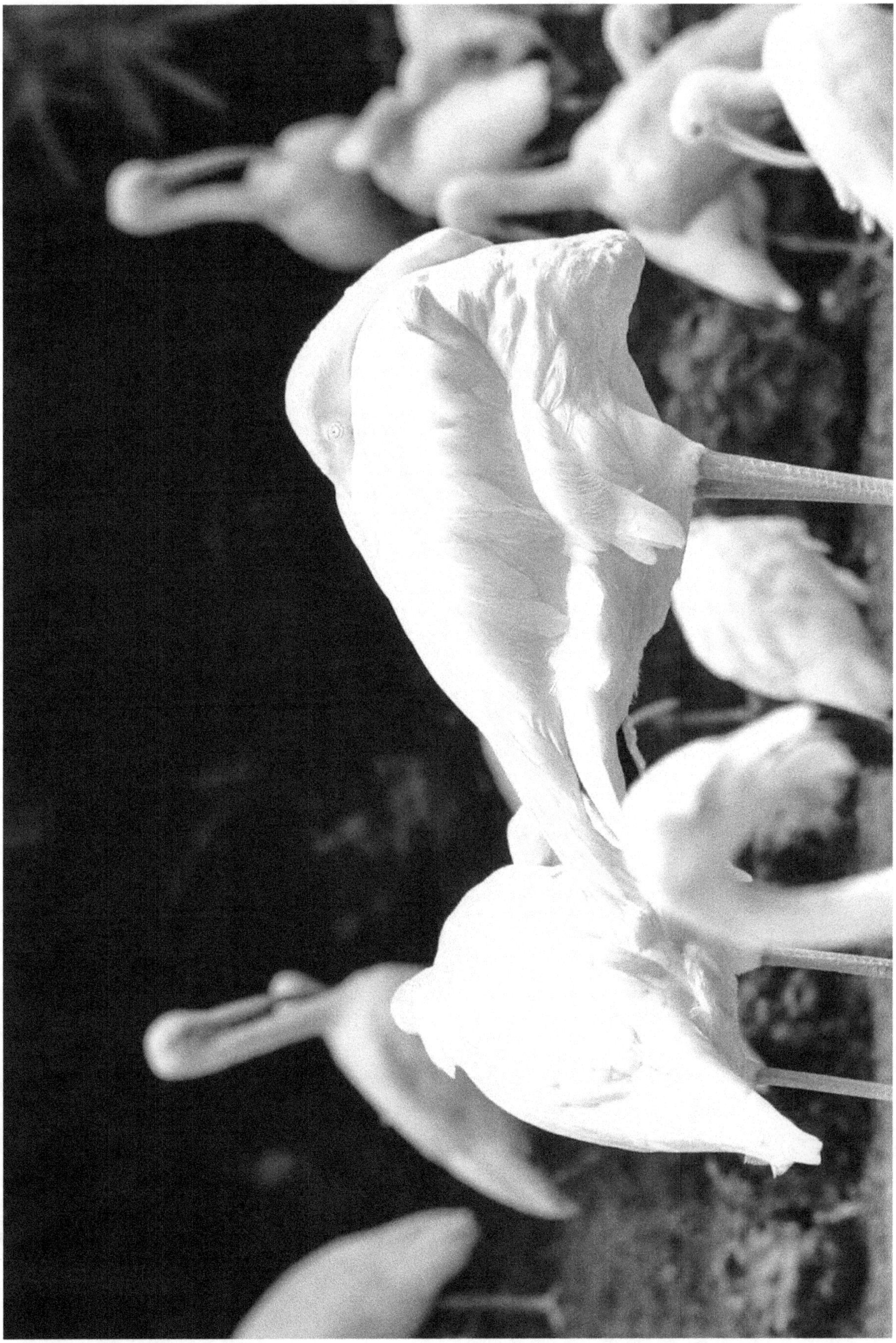

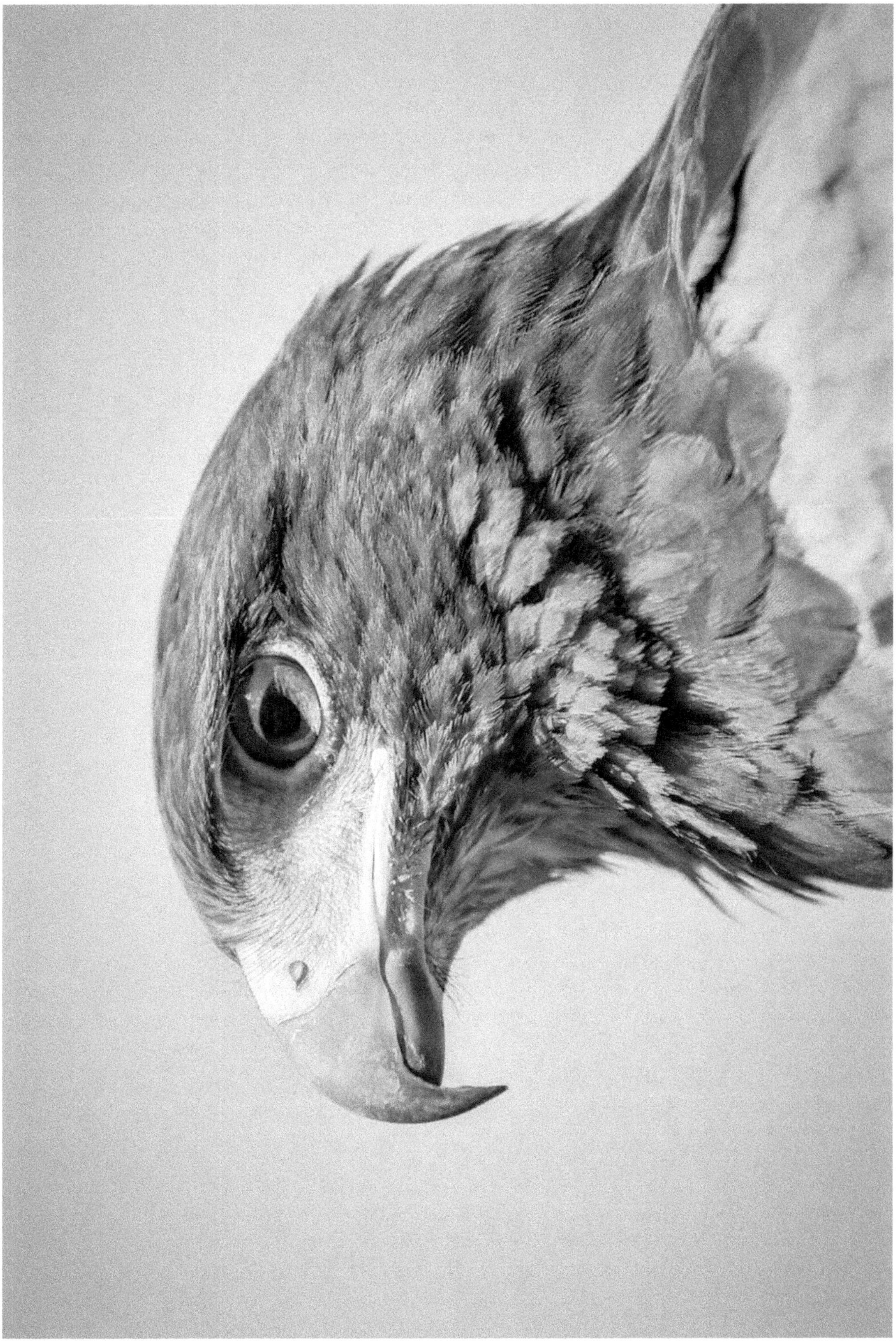

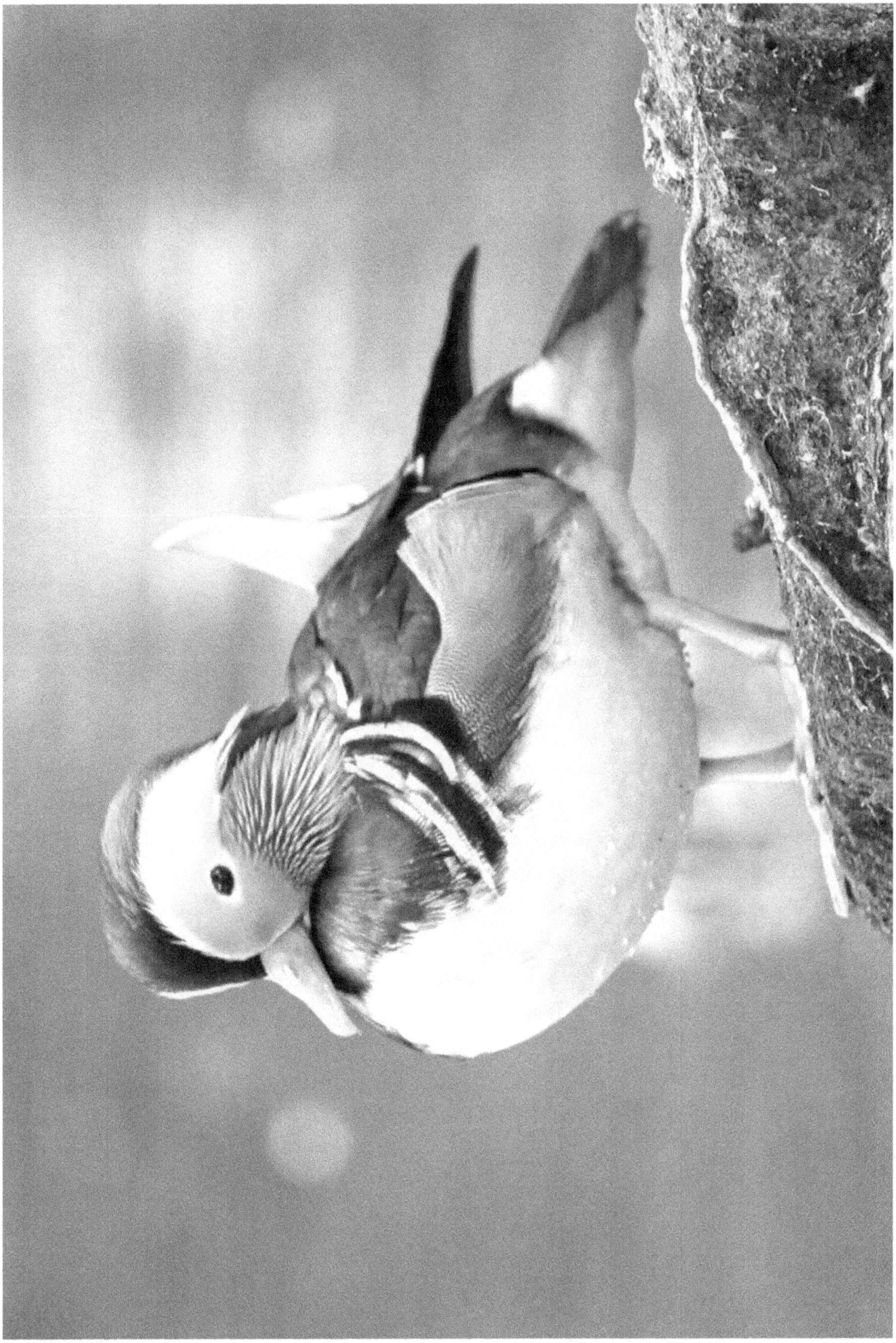

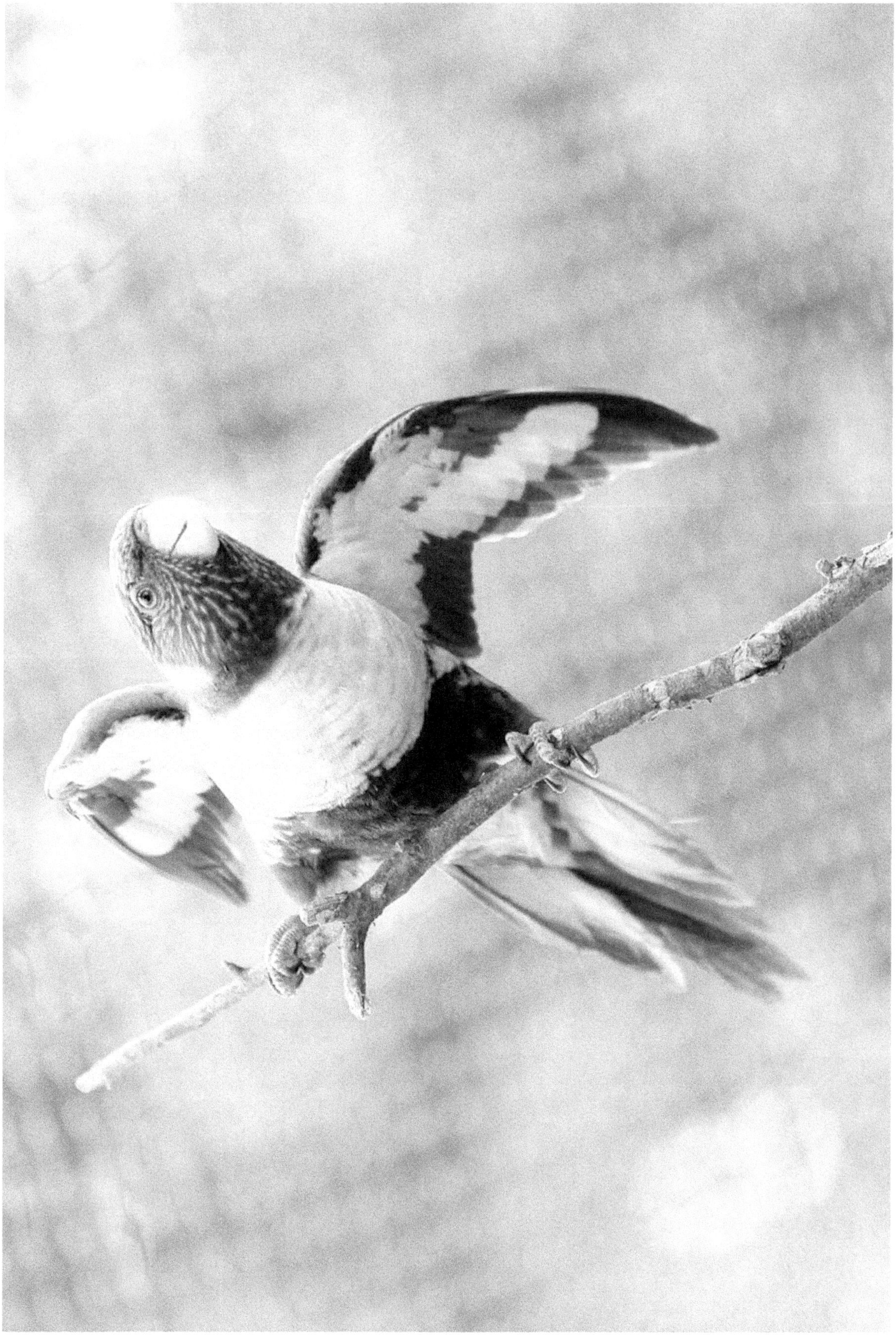

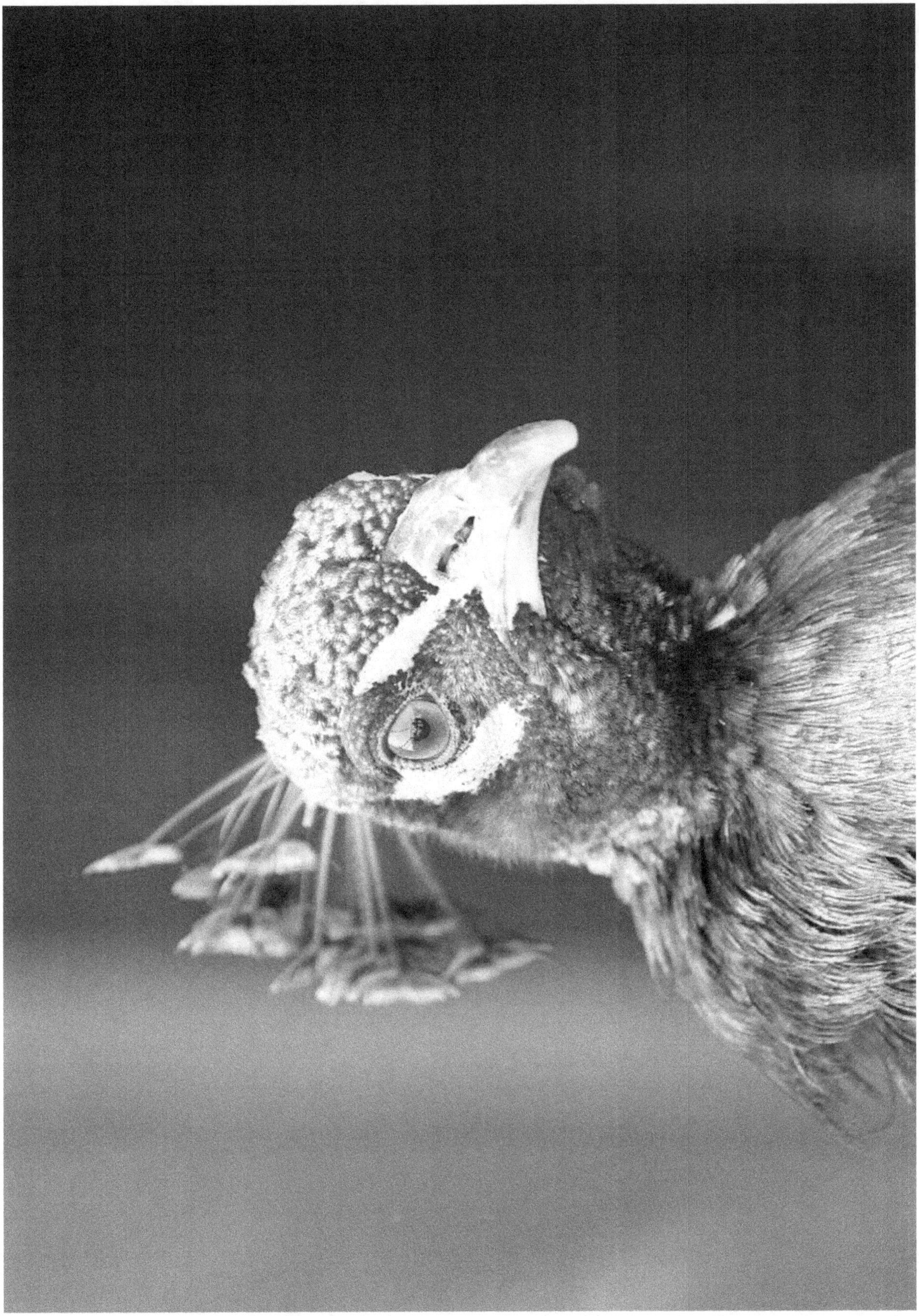

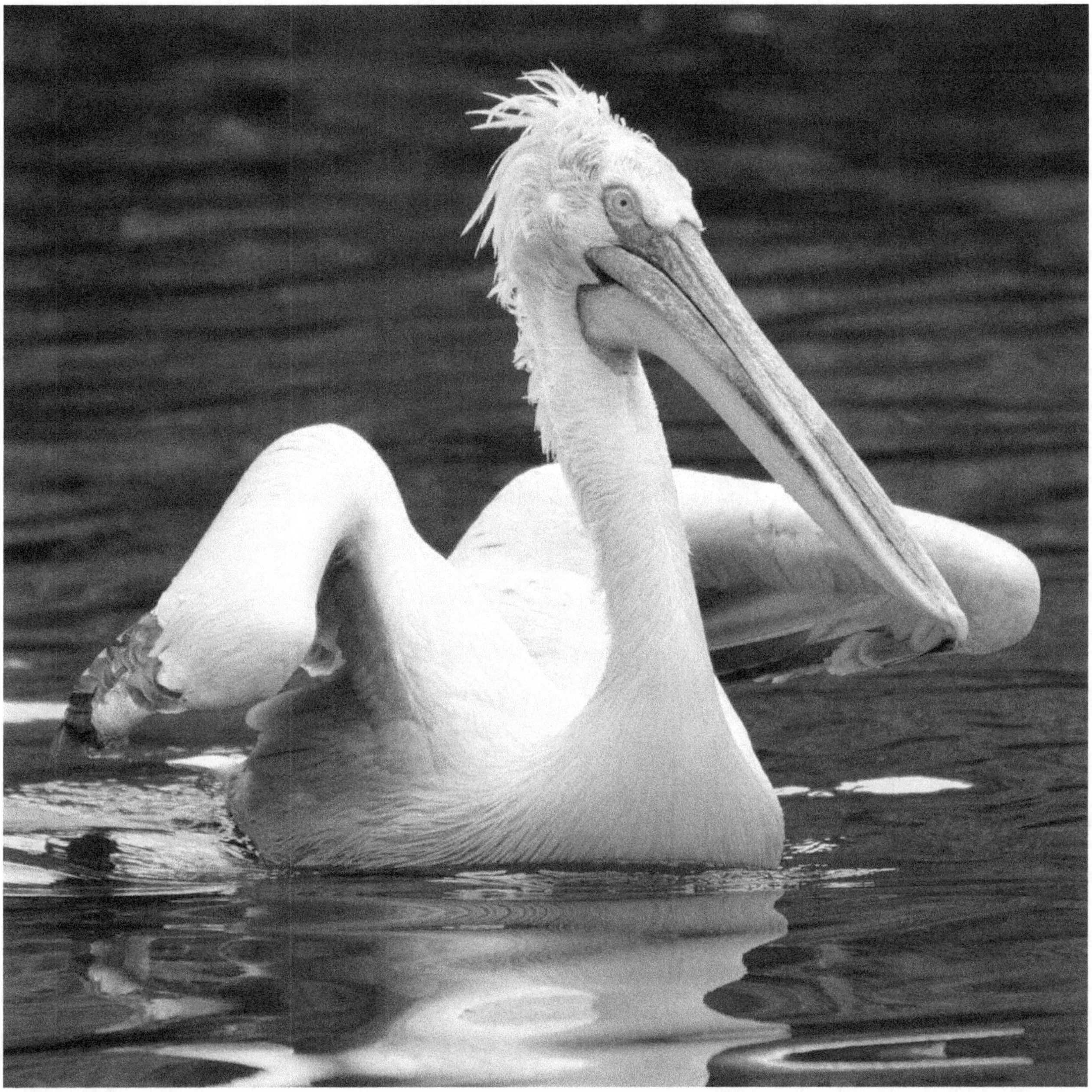

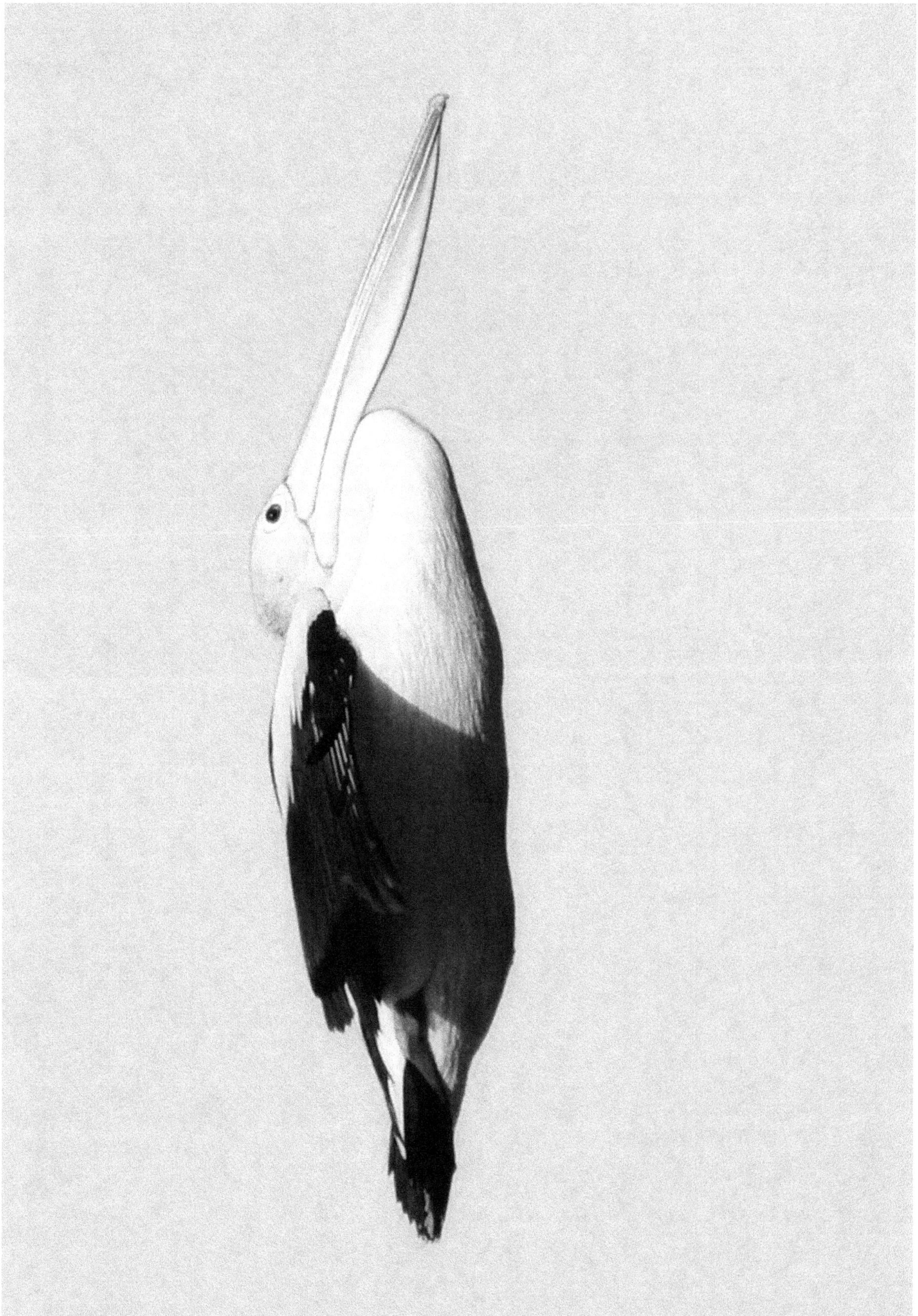

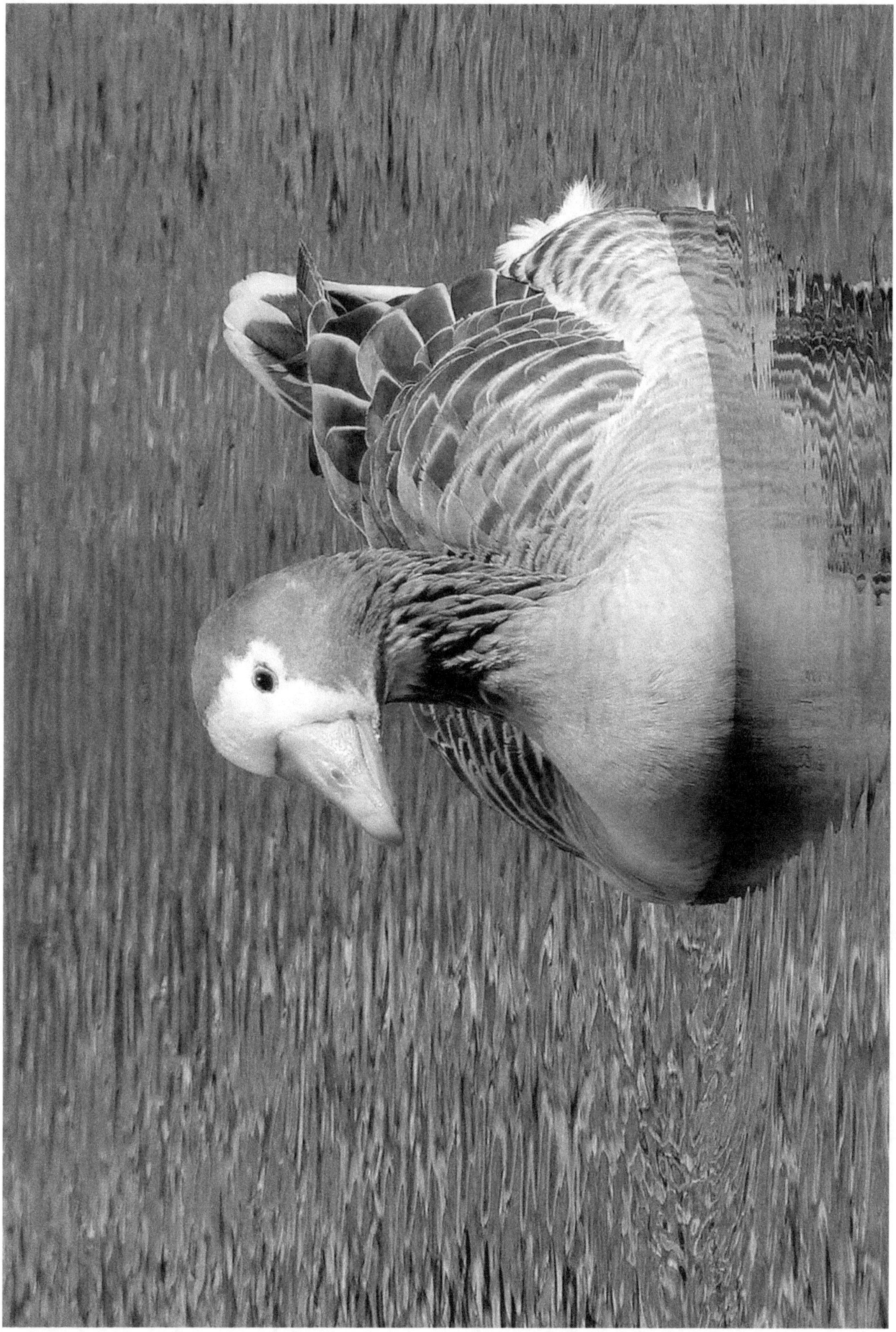

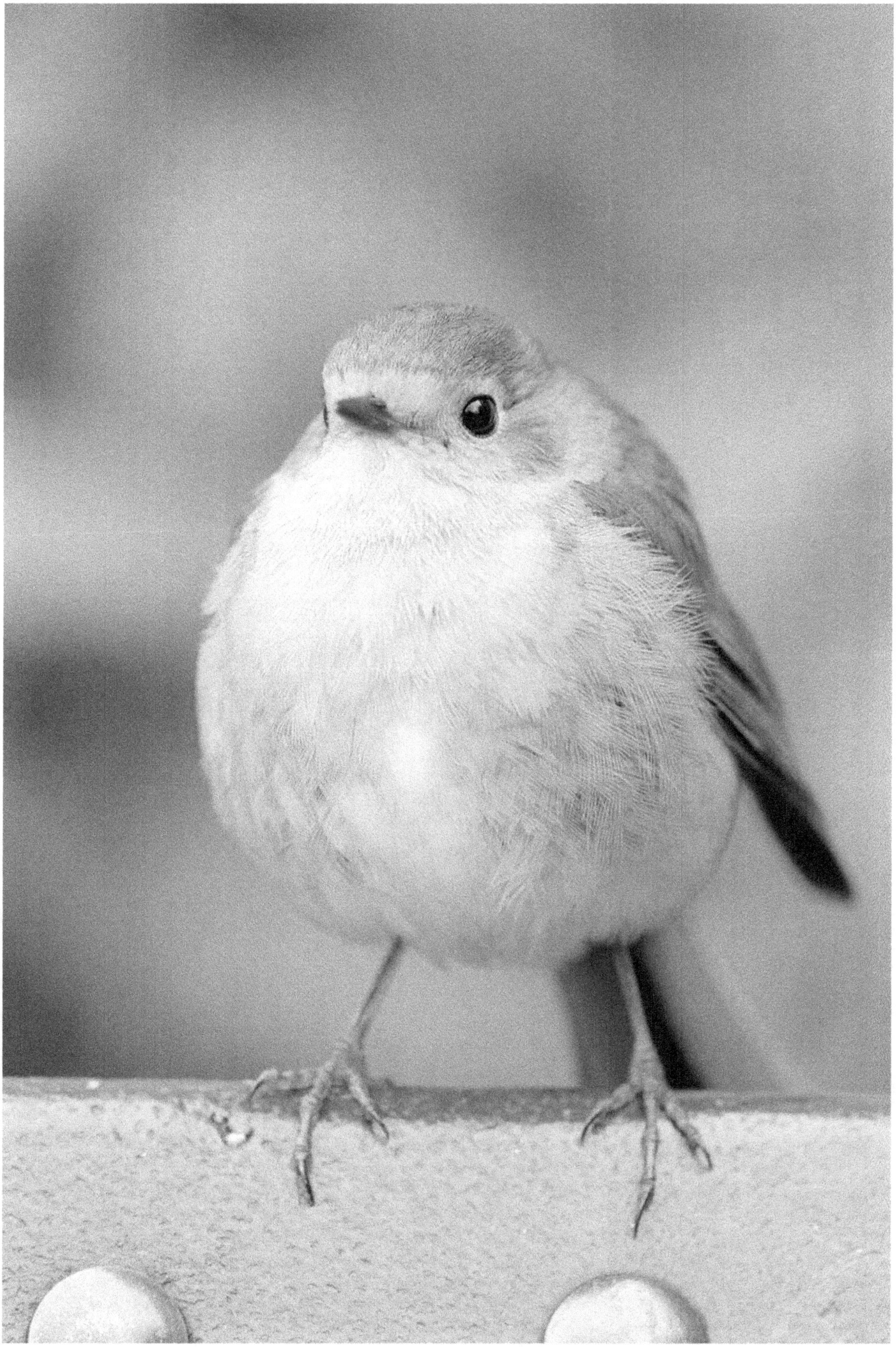

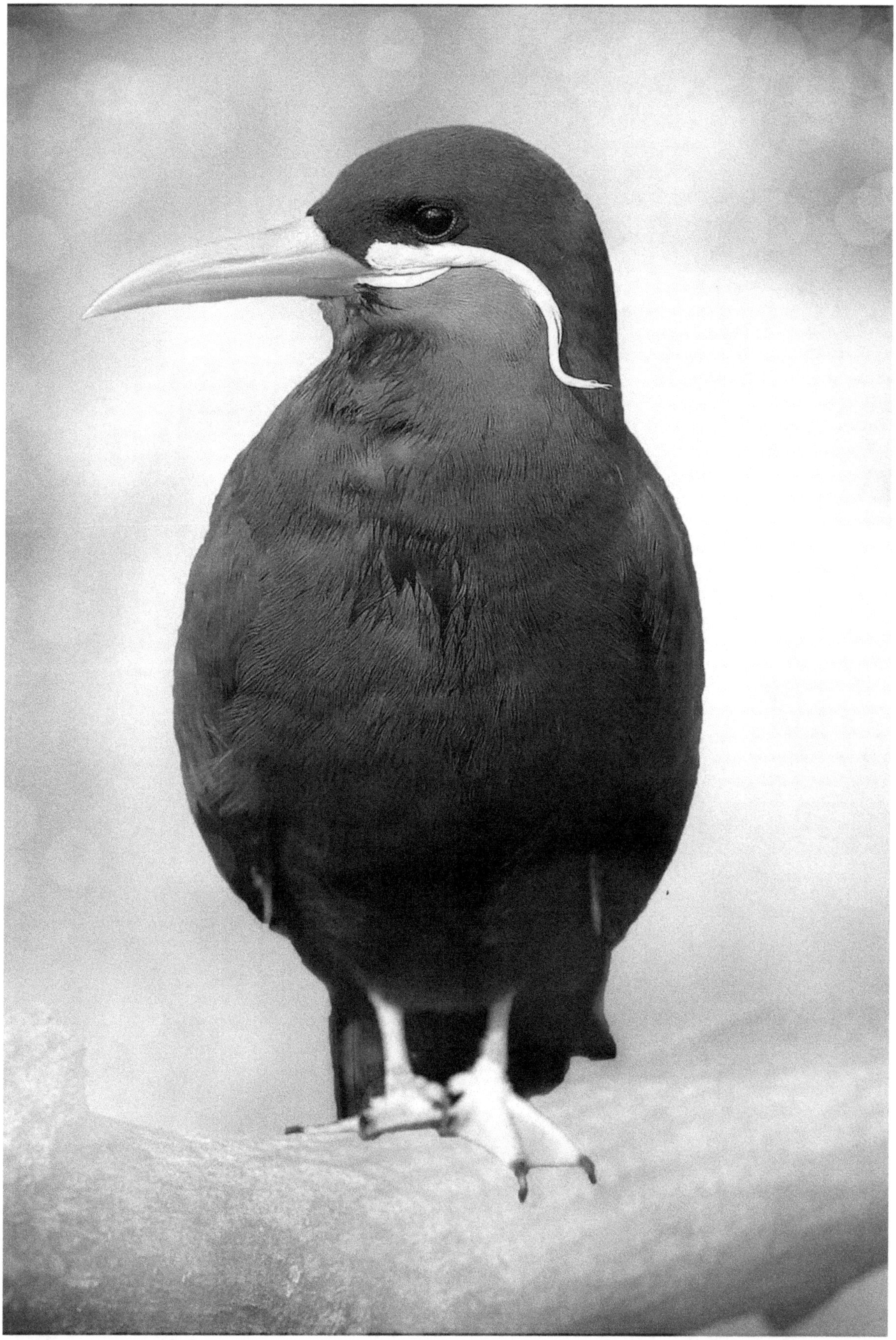

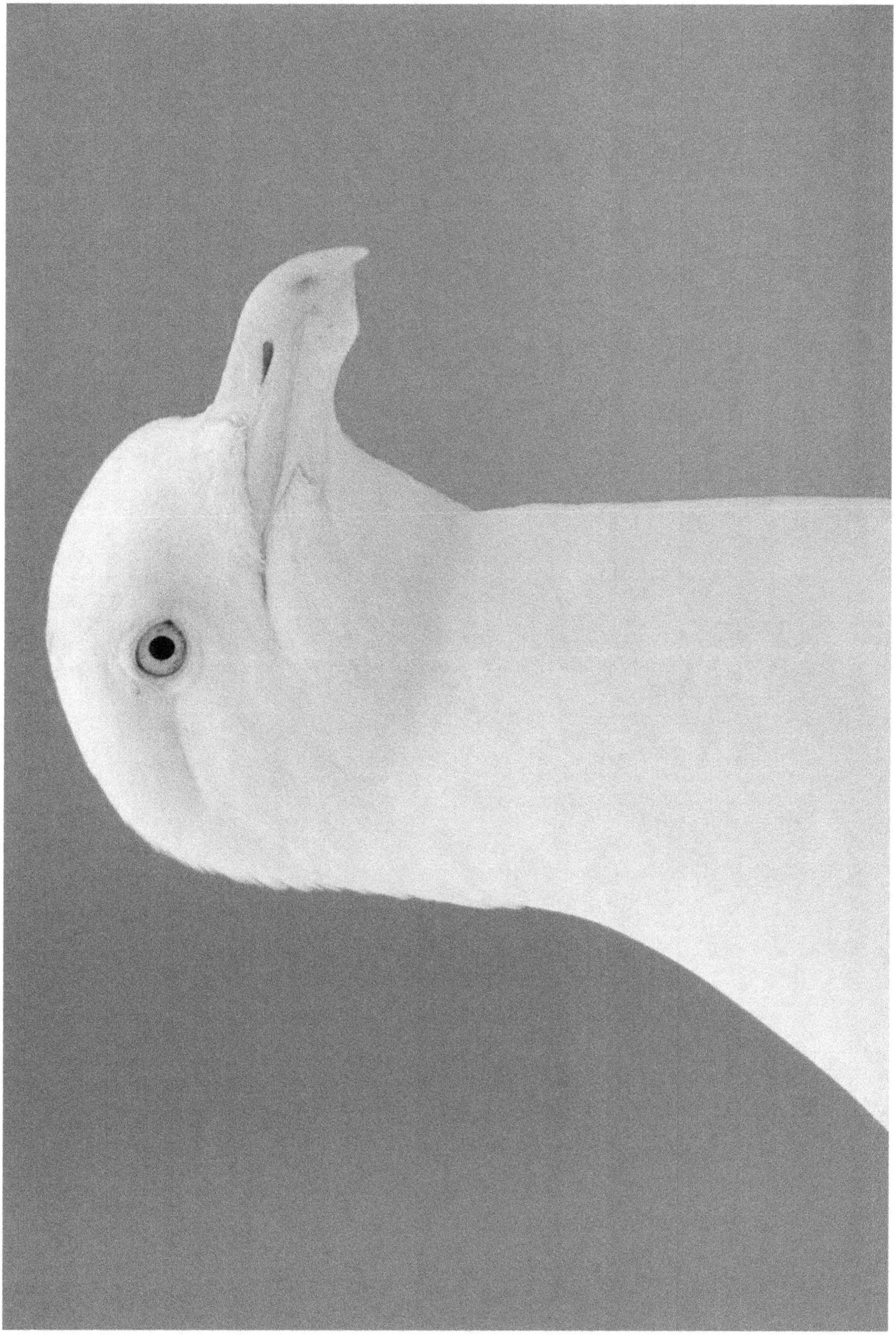

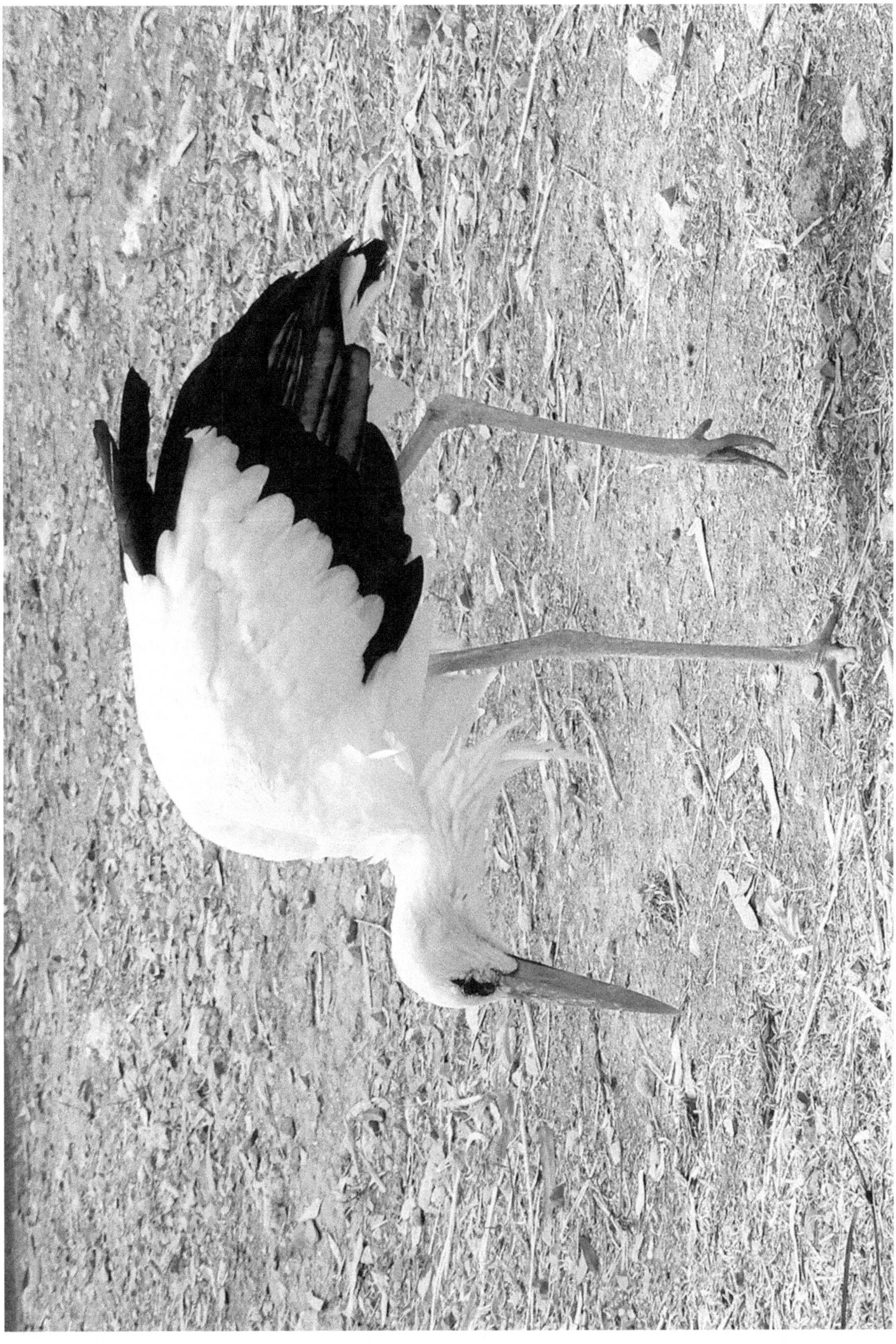

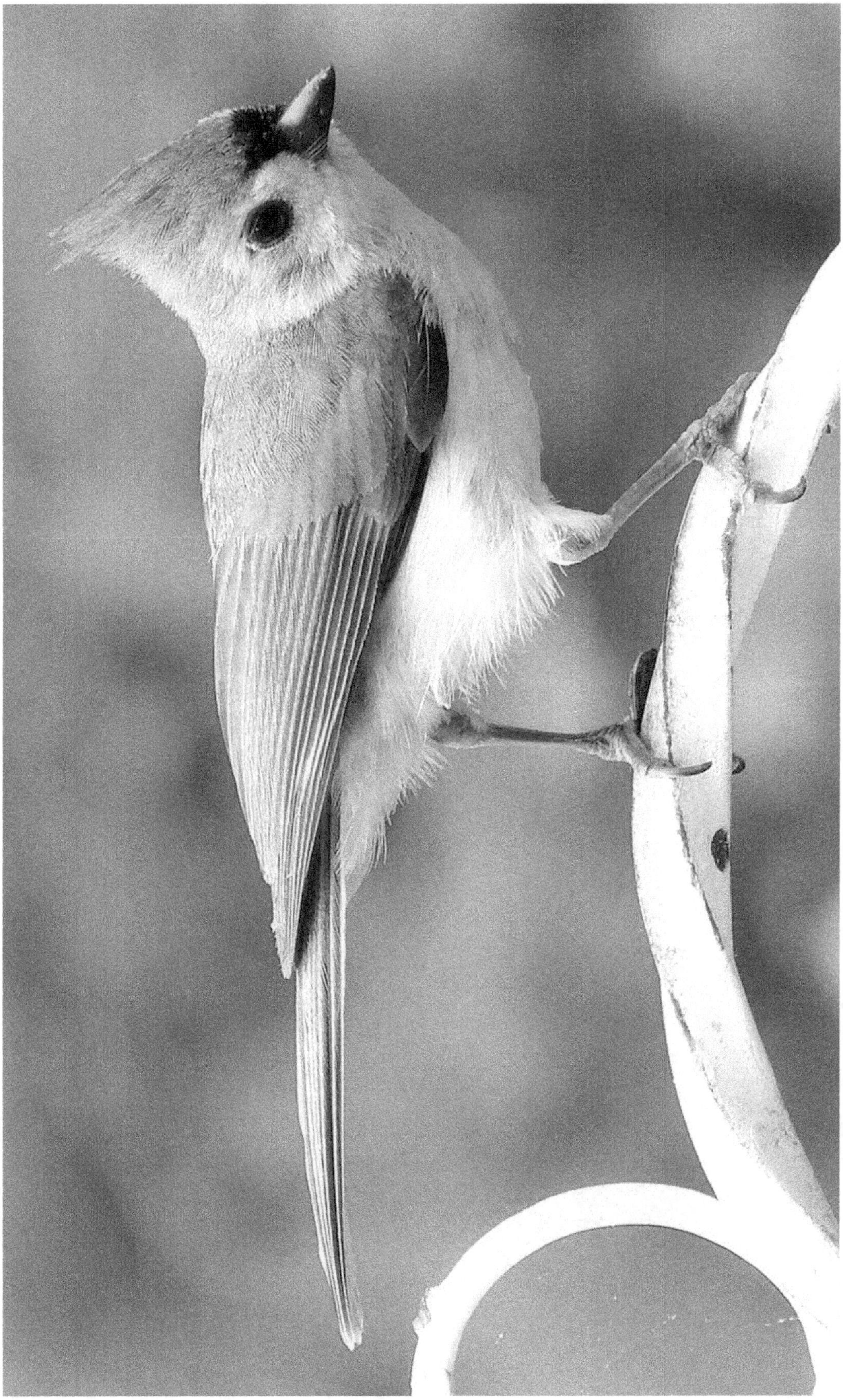

www.ingramcontent.com/pod-product-compliance
Lightning Source LLC
Chambersburg PA
CBHW080556190526
45169CB00007B/2796
9781535252935